A Little Cookbook

Rafi Fernandez
illustrated by Rosemary Woods

First published in 1992 by
The Appletree Press Ltd, 19-21 Alfred Street,
Belfast, BT2 8DL

Tel: ++44 (0) 1232 243074
Fax: ++44 (0) 1232 246756

email: frontdesk@appletree.ie
website address: www.irelandseye.com

A Little Balti Cookbook

9 8 7 6 5 4

Introduction

"Namaste", which means "hello", "goodbye", or even "how are you?" denotes gentle respect. The folded hands indicate the grace and welcome to be encountered all over India. The mystery and beauty of India is 5000 years old; land peopled by a hundred races, speaking a hundred tongues. Give each its due cultural and religious influences and let the centuries roll on to provide a rich profusion of eating habits, each a little different, each just a little more exotic than the other. The unforgettable aroma of India is not just the heavy scent of jasmine and roses. It is also the fragrance of the spices that are so important to Indian cooking. Although the word "curry" is an English derivative of *kari* (which means spice sauce), today, with Indians widely spread in western countries, some good commercial curry powders and pastes are available on the market. These are usually blends of spices such as turmeric, cardamom, ginger, coriander, nutmeg, cinnamon and many more. Indian *Bawarchis* (master chefs), however, using their own individual spice mixes, create dishes as artists use a palette of colours. No other country can provide such a diverse spectrum of foods or promise a gastronomic adventure quite like India.

Baltistan is a region situated in the northern-most part of Pakistan. Its cuisine has become popular in western countries, and *balti* restaurants now abound. Baltistanis are Muslims, and a hardy mountain people. Their dishes are generally cooked in a *balti*, a cast-iron pot with two handles whose hemispherical shape evolved from the Chinese wok. Any cooking technique can be used and the food has a unique quality.

The Modern Indian Kitchen

Today several commercial brands offer prepared *masalas* (blended spice mix) in powder and paste form and I find these a great boon. Test different brands to find your preference.

Varieties of *masala* mixes

Kashmiri	Mild or hot curry
Green	Madras
Garam	Pasanda
Tikka	Bhuna
Tandoori	Roghan Josh
Kebab	Vindaloo
Biryani	Dhansak
Balti	Korma

Other useful pastes

If possible, obtain the following pastes in Indian or Chinese brands as they are pure, with no additives. Once opened, they will keep in the fridge for up to three weeks or they can be divided into portions and frozen.

Ginger	Garlic
Coriander	Red or green chilli

Other ingredients

Commercial deep-fried onion is a great time saver (2oz/50g = 1 large raw onion). Curry leaves (*Kariyapath*) and coriander leaves (*Kotmir*) are available, fresh or dried. (Fresh leaves can be washed, dried and open-frozen.) Ingredients used in the book are widely available from groceries and supermarkets and can be obtained by mail order from various sources.

Coconut milk (*Nariyal doodh*) is available in tins, powder form or in cream blocks. To obtain 6 fl oz/175ml thick coconut milk add 3oz/75g coconut cream to 6 fl oz/175ml boiling water. To obtain 6 fl oz/175ml thin coconut milk, add 1 oz/25g coconut cream to 6 fl oz/175ml boiling water.

Gram flour is flour made from split peas. *Gram* or *dhals* are pulses — red lentils, moong beans, and so on. The former is the whole grain seed and the latter come in split form and are sometimes washed and husked.

Khushka/Chawal

Plain Boiled Rice

Freshly-boiled rice is cooked daily all over India but favoured more in South India. Rice, the ancient sages of India believed, is a gift of the gods, and its preparation is a form of prayer.

---

12 oz/350g/1 1/2 cups Patna or Basmati rice
18 fl oz/500ml/3 cups water
1 tsp butter, vegetable or olive oil
1/2 tsp salt or to taste

Pick and wash the rice in several changes of water. Allow to soak for 30 minutes (if possible) for fluffier, cooked grains. Drain well and put the rice in a heavy pan which has a tight-fitting lid. Add the measured water, butter or oil and salt. Bring to boil, turn the heat to very low, cover and cook for 12–15 minutes. To serve, loosen the rice with a flat slotted spoon to release the steam and prevent damaging the grains.

Bhaghara Khushka (Pulao Rice)

First sauté the drained rice in butter or oil with $1/2$ tsp black cumin seeds, I in piece of cinnamon stick, 2 green cardamoms and 2 bay leaves. Add the water and salt and proceed as for plain boiled rice.

When the rice is cooked, lift the lid and pour the food colour of your choice mixed in a little milk on the surface of the rice at random. Cover the pan and rest for 5 minutes before serving as above. Garnish with browned onions and almond flakes.

Naan

Leavened Bread

The variety of Indian breads is infinite but the *naan* is by far the most popular one in the western world. Although, traditionally, they are baked in a *tandoor* (clay oven), they are just as delicious baked in an ordinary oven.

I tsp sugar	I tsp salt
I tsp fresh or dried yeast	I egg yolk beaten or
5 fl oz/150ml warm water	a little milk
8oz/200g plain flour	2 tsp poppy/onion/sesame
3oz/75g melted ghee or	seeds (or mixed)
unsalted butter	

Place the sugar, yeast and warm water in a cup. Whisk well and rest until it turns frothy. Sieve the flour and salt. Make a well and pour in the yeast mixture along with the *ghee* or butter. Mix together with your fingers. Now rub your palms with a little *ghee* or butter and make a smooth and soft dough. Knead for about 5 minutes. Rest dough covered for 2 hours

8

or more to rise. Divide into 6 portions and gently roll out on a lightly floured surface. Brush with egg or milk and sprinkle on the seeds. Place on greased baking tray and bake for 10–15 minutes in a pre-heated oven gas mark 8, 450°F, 230°C. Serve immediately or keep warm wrapped in tinfoil.

Gosht Biryani

Rice Layered with Meat

Id-ul-Fitr marks the end of the Ramazan fast at the appearance of the new moon. Fitr means five pounds of grain which is distributed to the poor. Biryani is truly a jewel made for a royal treat and therefore a favourite with the Noobs of Hyderabad. Served with Egg and Tomato Curry (p. 40) and a raitha (p. 12), it cannot fail to please.

5 fl oz/150ml milk	1 tsp turmeric powder
1 sachet saffron powder	salt to taste and 1 tsp sugar
6 tbsp lemon juice	2 lbs/900g cubed lamb or boned
4 green chillies, finely chopped	chicken
4 oz/100g fresh coriander, chopped	1 lb/450g Basmati rice
	1 tsp black cumin seeds
5 fl oz/150ml natural yogurt, beaten	4 green cardamoms
	2 in cinnamon stick
4 tbsp biryani masala	6 tbsp melted ghee or unsalted
2 tbsp garam masala	butter

Mix the milk and saffron and keep aside. Mix the next 8 items and marinade the lamb or chicken in it for 4–6 hours. Gently cook it for 45 minutes in a heavy pan. Meanwhile, wash the rice and cook with whole spices in boiling water until the grains are a quarter done. Drain.

Grease the base of a heavy pan and place half the rice in an even but loose layer. Spread the cooked meat mixture with all the juices over the rice. Spread the remaining rice over this in a loose neat layer. Pour the saffron milk over the rice at random spots. Finally pour the *ghee* or butter over the rice. Grease a circular piece of foil (the size of the pan) and place it greased side down on the rice. Cover the pan and cook on low to medium heat for about 20 minutes or until the rice is fluffy. Gently toss the rice and meat together before serving.

Raitha

Yogurt, Mint and Cucumber Salad

---

10 fl oz/300ml natural yogurt, beaten
2 tsp mint sauce (or to taste)
salt and sugar to taste
4oz/100g cucumber, thinly sliced
$^1/_2$ tsp paprika
fresh mint leaves for garnish

Mix the first four ingredients gently together and chill. Garnish with paprika and mint leaves and serve.

Roghan Josh

Lamb in a Deep Red Sauce

A visit to Kashmir is incomplete until you have stayed on a houseboat on the beautiful Dal lake and eaten meals cooked by the *khansaba* (cook) on the kitchen boat which travels alongside the main houseboat.

---

1 tbsp ghee *or vegetable oil*	8–10 saffron strands *or*
1/2 tsp asafoetida powder	1 sachet powdered saffron
1 lb/450g cubed lean lamb	1/2 tsp sugar
5 fl oz/150ml natural yogurt	salt to taste
beaten with 1/2 tsp cornflour	4 tbsp tomato purée
2 tbsp roghan josh	blanched almond flakes
1 tsp kashmiri masala	for garnish
1 tsp garam masala	

Heat the *ghee* or oil in a heavy pan and fry the asafoetida and lamb on a medium heat until the meat pieces are sealed. Remove from the heat and cool a little. Fold in the yogurt and return to the heat and cook until the yogurt is absorbed. Add the remaining ingredients except the garnish and cook until the meat is tender and the gravy almost dry. Garnish with the almond flakes and serve hot. If you prefer a hotter curry (*phaal*), then add 2 tsp chilli powder with the *masalas* to the above recipe and you will achieve the hottest curry available in restaurants.

Rafi's Paretal

Dry Meat Curry

This recipe is dedicated to all my pupils who love it, especially Peter who made double batches in his wok that looked like a volcano erupting. It is truly a "Rafi" invention for those who like it hot.

---

1 1/2 tsp chilli powder (or adjust to taste)
2 tbsp madras curry powder
1 tsp turmeric powder
salt to taste
3 tbsp vegetable oil
2 large onions, finely sliced
2 tsp ginger, garlic and chilli paste
8 curry leaves
1 lb/450g cubed lean lamb or beef
6 fl oz/175ml thick coconut milk (p. 7)
8oz/200g tinned chopped tomatoes

Mix the first 4 ingredients with 6 tablespoons water to a smooth paste. Heat the oil in a heavy pan and fry the onions until golden brown. Add the ginger, garlic and chilli paste, curry leaves and the spice paste and fry until the oil rises above the *masala*. Add the meat and fry until evenly sealed. Lower the heat, cover the pan and simmer for about 45 minutes. Add the coconut milk and tomatoes and mix well. Simmer gently until the meat is fully cooked. Serve hot with plain rice.

Balti Surmahi Gosht

Lamb with Fenugreek Leaves

Balti people are mainly meat eaters, chiefly goat or mutton which require long, slow cooking. Lamb requires less cooking time but a slow simmer will provide the aromatic and tasty result.

2lb/900g lamb, cubed	2 tbsp balti masala
5 green cardamoms	4oz/100g kasoori methi
2 black cardamoms	(dried fenugreek leaves)
6 cloves	$^1/_2$ tsp each fennel, nigella
2"/5cm piece cinnamon stick	and onion seeds
4 bay leaves	$^1/_2$ tsp turmeric, cumin and
Purée:	coriander powder
1 large onion	salt to taste
2oz/50g fresh ginger	4 fresh tomatoes, finely chopped
6 cloves garlic	(reserve 1 for garnish)

Place the lamb and whole spices in a *balti*, or heavy pan, and cover with cold water. Bring to the boil and simmer until the water has nearly evaporated, skimming any froth if necessary. Fold in the spice purée, mix well, and gently simmer until the lamb is fully cooked and the gravy thick, about 45 minutes – 1 hour. Garnish with chopped tomato.

Balti Bhuna Chammp

Lamb Chops with Lentils

Cooking lamb or mutton with lentils to give extra body is popular in Balti cooking. This dish has a sourish tang with the herbal overtones of an array of spices.

4oz/100g bengal gram (channa dhal)
1 large onion, finely sliced
2oz/50g fresh ginger
4 cloves garlic, crushed
2lb/900g lamb chops, excess fat trimmed
1/2 tsp each turmeric and cumin powder
4 bay leaves
2 tbsp oil
4 ripe tomatoes, finely chopped
5 green chillies, left whole or chopped
2 tbsp bhuna masala
1 tsp garam masala
salt to taste
generous handful of fresh coriander, coarsely chopped

Place the first seven ingredients in a *balti* or heavy pan and cover with cold water. Bring to the boil and simmer until the *dhal* is soft and most of the water has evaporated. In a small frying pan, heat the oil and fry the remaining ingredients until well blended. Add this together with the oil to the lamb and *dhal* and mix well. Simmer for a further 10 minutes. Serve hot with *naan* or boiled rice.

Galina Xacutti

Goan Chicken

It is difficult, with just one recipe, to lead you into the sanctum of Goan (now Panjim) cuisine. The method of eating is both a meal and a ritual. The local men start drinking *feni*, a potent cashew liquor, in the afternoon to set the pace and mood for the pungent and spicy food that follows.

6oz/150g/½ cup desiccated coconut	2 onions, finely sliced
2 tsp each cumin, coriander and mustard seeds	1 tsp turmeric
4 cloves garlic and 1 in fresh ginger	salt to taste and a pinch of sugar
4 cloves and 8 peppercorns	3 lb/1.5 kg chicken, skinned and jointed
6 whole dry red chillies	9 fl oz/250ml thick coconut milk
1 tsp five-spice powder	4 tbsp tomato purée
1 onion, chopped	1 tsp freshly-grated nutmeg
4 tbsp oil	

Dry-roast the first 7 items in a frying pan until the onion and desiccated coconut are a deep golden brown. Grind all of these in a processor to a smooth paste and reserve. Heat the oil and fry the sliced onions until brown. Add the *masala* paste, turmeric and salt. Fry for 2–3 minutes. Add the chicken and remaining ingredients. Bring to the boil, then simmer until the chicken is cooked and the gravy is thick.

Mulligatawny

Anglo-Indian Stew

An Indian mini-Amsterdam, Cochin is a complex of islands and towns linked by bridges and ferries influenced by the past — Dutch — and the present. The original *mulla-ga-tani* changed, through the Dutch influence, with addition of meats, coconut milk and tomatoes.

---

1 pt/600ml chicken or vegetable stock
1 onion, finely chopped
8 oz/200g fresh or tinned tomatoes, chopped
1 tsp each garlic and ginger paste
2 in/2.5 cm cinnamon stick
6–8 curry leaves
1 tsp each coriander and cumin powder
$1/2$ tsp fenugreek powder or 8–10 fenugreek seeds
9 fl oz/250ml thick coconut milk
3 lb/1.5 kg boned chicken pieces or
2 lb/900g raw king prawns, shelled and deveined
1 onion, finely sliced and deep-fried
4 tbsp lemon juice
salt to taste
a handful of fresh coriander leaves, chopped

Place the first 10 items in a large pan and bring to the boil. Simmer for about 10 minutes. Add the chicken or prawns and simmer until they are cooked (prawns require less cooking time). Fold in the remaining ingredients and serve hot.

Balti Pathani Murgh

Moghul Style Chicken

The men of Baltistan always carry a 'balti' in their back packs while herding and can achieve delicious dishes made with pheasants, guinea fowls, partridges or quails even in the harshest mountains. This recipe has been adapted for chicken.

3oz/75g deep-fried onions	1½ tbsp biryani masala
2oz/50g each ginger and garlic crushed	1 tsp kashmiri masala or chopped fresh chillies to taste
½ tsp each fenugreek, fennel and nigella seeds	salt to taste
4 green cardamoms	14oz/400g chopped tomatoes drained (reserve juice)
2 black cardamoms	3lb/900g chicken breasts, skinned and cut into large pieces
2 star anise	
2"/5cm piece of cinnamon	7 fl oz/200ml fromage frais or natural yogurt, beaten
2 bay leaves	
2oz/50g ground almonds	few fresh mint leaves for garnish

Place all the ingredients except the last three in a *balti* or a large heavy pan and gently heat, stirring constantly, until all the ingredients are well mixed and the onions have dissolved, about 10–15 minutes. Add the chicken and mix well. Cover and cook until the chicken is tender, about 30 minutes. Cool the curry and gradually fold in the *fromage frais* or yogurt, stirring regularly to avoid curdling. Reheat gently and, if the sauce is too thick, add some of the reserved tomato juice. Garnish with mint leaves.

Balti Baingan

Stuffed Aubergine Curry

Though Baltistan does not have a very wide range of vegetables, curries cooked with what is available are mouthwatering. This curry has a hot and tangy taste and is best served with rice and *tarka dhal* (see p. 00).

1 tsp each coriander, cumin and turmeric powder	4 tbsp oil
	1 tsp cumin seeds
½ tsp chilli powder (or to taste)	**Purée:**
1 tsp amchur *(dry mango powder)* or 2 tbsp lemon juice or vinegar	1 large onion
	2 green chillies (or to taste)
2 cloves garlic, finely crushed	1 tsp balti masala
salt to taste	2oz/50g ground almonds
9oz/250g baby aubergines	or cashew nuts
or 2 large ones	1 tsp sugar

Mix all the spice powders, garlic and salt to a smooth paste with a little water (if using lemon juice or vinegar this will suffice). Make cross slits on top of the aubergines, about 1"/2½cm deep. Stuff the spice paste into the slits. Heat the oil in a *balti* or a deep frying pan and fry the cumin seeds and aubergines until the skins produce white spots. Turn the aubergines several times so they are evenly fried. Remove, leaving any oil in the pan, and keep warm. Reheat the oil gently and fry the purée for about 5 minutes. Replace the aubergines and any juice and mix well. Cover and cook on a low heat, stirring gently occasionally, until the aubergines are cooked and the oil has separated. If the mixture is too dry add a little hot water to avoid burning.

Murgh ka Salan

Bhori-style Chicken

Festive Muslim *bhori* dinners are served on the floor on a *dastar khan* — a white linen cloth which has been delicately decorated with raw grains, flower petals and greenery. When the meal is over, all of the decorations are thrown into a river, lake or well.

4 tbsp vegetable oil	3 lb/1.5 kg chicken (remove
2 medium onions, finely sliced	skin and bone if you wish)
1 tsp garam masala	2 tbsp tomato purée
4 tsp bhuna masala	9 fl oz/275g tinned tomatoes
1 tsp turmeric powder	6 fl oz/175ml thick
5 fl oz/150ml water	coconut milk (p. 7)
	salt to taste

Heat the oil and fry the onions until golden brown. In the meantime mix the *masalas* and turmeric with the water. When the onions are brown add the *masalas* and fry for 3–5 minutes. Add the chicken and fry until evenly coloured. Add the remaining ingredients, mix well, lower the heat and cook covered until the chicken is done. Serve hot. (Fold in $1/2$ tsp sugar if you wish before serving.)

Dhansak

Hot, Sweet and Sour Potpourri

Parsis came to India from Persia bringing their own culinary genius. A reporter found a young student who read the newspaper marriage columns and thereby attended 150 Parsi feasts during his 3 years at university in Bombay.

2oz/50g each red gram (tuwar), Bengal gram (channa)
green gram (moong) and red lentils (masoor)
4 fresh mint leaves or 1/2 tsp mint sauce
12 fl oz/350ml water
I large aubergine, potato and carrot
4oz/100g deep-fried onions
I oz/25g dried fenugreek leaves
4 tbsp vegetable oil
3 tsp each of ginger, garlic, green chilli paste
3 tbsp dhansak masala
4oz/100g fresh coriander, chopped
I lb/450g chicken portions or raw king prawns
4 tbsp lemon juice
salt to taste and I tsp sugar

Place the first 6 items in a heavy pan and bring to the boil. Simmer until the lentils and vegetables are soft and can be mashed with a wooden spoon. Reserve. In a separate pan heat the oil and fry the spices and *masala*, coriander and chicken pieces. When the chicken pieces are sealed add the lentil and vegetable sauce and simmer until the chicken is cooked. Add the lemon juice and seasoning and serve hot with *Baghara Khushka* (p. 8). If you use prawns, reduce the cooking time.

Porcheri

South Indian Vegetable Stew

Udipi, Vihar and Bhavan are generic names for South Indian vegetarian restaurants where food is served on banana leaves. As you unfold the banana leaf and get ready to eat, remember to sprinkle your leaf with water from the glass already set out. The waiter will not serve you until this cleansing ritual has been completed.

8oz/200g Bengal gram (channa dhal)
400g/1 lb cut mixed vegetables of your choice
1 1/2 tsp chilli powder
1 tsp turmeric powder
salt to taste
2 tsp soft brown sugar
8oz/200g desiccated coconut
4 tbsp coconut or vegetable oil
1 tsp each mustard and cumin seeds
6–8 curry leaves

Cook the *dhal* with plenty of water until soft. Drain and reserve the water. Gently mash the *dhal* with a wooden spoon and keep aside. Cook the vegetables in the reserved water with chilli and turmeric powder, salt, sugar and half the coconut. When the vegetables are done add the *dhal* and gently fold together. Heat the oil and fry the seeds, curry leaves and remaining coconut until the coconut is light brown. Pour all this over the vegetable and *dhal* and mix well. Reheat the whole mixture and serve hot.

Gucci Mattar Paneer

Mushroom, Peas and Cheese Curry

In Rajasthan *Teej Mala* (Festival of Devi) is essentially for women and in particular mothers and their daughters-in-law. Devi, the wife of Lord Shiva, is worshipped for two days to obtain her gratitude and to give her adoration. Only vegetarian dishes are cooked by the daughters-in-law to remain in the grace and favour of the mothers-in-law. Feta can be used as a substitute for *paneer*.

Purée:	4 tbsp ghee *or vegetable oil*
8oz/200g tinned tomatoes	I tsp nigella seeds (ajwain)
I tsp each ginger and garlic paste	8oz/200g button mushrooms, halved
6 green chillies	8oz/200g garden peas
I tsp pasanda masala	8oz/200g paneer, *cubed and fried until golden*
6 fl oz/150ml double cream	
¹/2 tsp cornflour	handful of fresh coriander leaves, chopped
I small onion	

Heat the *ghee* or oil and fry the nigella seeds. Add the puréed *masala* and sauté over medium heat stirring constantly. Fold in the mushrooms, peas and *paneer*. Simmer for 15 minutes. Garnish with the coriander leaves and serve hot.

Dahi-ni-Kari

Yogurt Curry

Masters of vegetarian cooking, Gujeratis make, in an endless procession, a variety of mouth-watering dishes from the simplest lentils and vegetables.

12oz/350g natural yogurt, beaten
4 fl oz/125ml thin coconut milk
4 tbsp gram flour mixed in $^1/_2$ cup water
$^1/_2$ tsp each turmeric and chilli powder
salt to taste and $^1/_2$ tsp sugar
10oz/280g corn kernels with peppers
4 tbsp vegetable oil
4 whole dried red chillies
1 tsp cumin seeds
2 cloves garlic, crushed
6–8 curry leaves
$^1/_4$ tsp asafoetida

Mix the first 5 items and pass through a sieve. Add corn and peppers and on a low heat cook the mixture until the sauce is smooth and thick. Set aside. Heat the oil and fry the remaining ingredients until the garlic turns golden brown. Pour the oil and spices over the yogurt sauce and cover the pan to infuse. Gently re-heat and serve plain or compliment with *Bhajias* (p. 43). If you are adding the *Bhajias* allow them to simmer in the curry for 5 minutes before serving.

Ande aur Tamatar ka Cut

Egg and Tomato Curry

This dish originated in the Deccan and the *Dakhnis* love their food hot. Traditionally served with *Biryani* (p. 11), you can add vegetables of your choice to make an even more wholesome dish.

$1\frac{1}{2}$ pts tomato juice
2 oz/50g coconut cream
4 tbsp gram flour (besan) *mixed in a little water*
2 tsp kashmiri masala
1 tsp garam masala
salt to taste and $\frac{1}{2}$ tsp sugar
2 tsp each vegetable oil and sesame oil
1 tsp cumin seeds
4 whole dried red chillies
6 curry leaves
4 cloves garlic, sliced
$\frac{1}{4}$ tsp asafoetida
4 hard-boiled eggs, halved
browned onions and fresh coriander for garnish

Mix the first 6 items in a large pan and gently heat until the coconut has dissolved. In a frying pan heat the oils and fry the remaining ingredients except the eggs and garnish. When the garlic slices are a deep golden brown, pour everything over the tomato mixture and cover to allow the spice aroma to infuse. Reheat gently, float the halved eggs on top and garnish with browned onions and coriander and serve hot.

Bhajias

Savoury Fritters

At Navratri, the festival of Nine Nights during which Durga, the warrior goddess, is worshipped, people only eat light snacks like *bhajias, samosas, pakoras*, etc. India seems to have more snacks than any other country in the world.

8oz/200g gram flour (besan or channa atta)
I tsp baking powder
salt to taste
$^1/_2$ tsp each turmeric and chilli powder
$^1/_2$ tsp each onion, nigella, cumin and fennel seeds, coarsely ground
2 green chillies, finely chopped
handful of fresh coriander leaves, chopped
2 large onions, finely sliced

Sieve the first 4 items in a large mixing bowl. Add the remaining ingredients and toss. Gradually add water and, using your hand, mix the ingredients in until you have folded in all the dry flour and have a thick dropping consistency batter. Heat sufficient oil for deep-frying and, when smoking hot, drop spoonfuls of the mixture and fry until golden brown. Drain well and serve or use in *Dahi-ni-Kari* (p. 39).

Balti Murgh Tikka Masala

Chicken Tikka in Gravy

Although Baltistan never became part of the Moghul kingdom, some Moghul culinary hints crept into its cuisine. Balti people love chicken and this is a very popular dish. The chicken is usually cooked on the bone but boning it will reduce cooking time.

---

4 tbsp tikka masala
4oz/125ml natural yogurt
salt to taste
pinch of sugar
4 chicken breasts, boned, skinned and cubed
Sauce:
2 tbsp korma masala
4oz/125ml natural yogurt, beaten
6 deep red fresh tomatoes, chopped
salt to taste
$^1/_2$ tsp sugar

Mix the first four ingredients and marinade the chicken for 1 hour, or longer if possible,. Put chicken on a mesh grid or on skewers and grill under medium heat. Baste chicken, turn over, and grill until well-cooked and slightly burnt. Keep hot. To make the sauce, mix all the ingredients in a *balti* or frying pan. Add all the juices collected in the grill tray. Gently heat, stirring constantly to avoid curdling. When the sauce is well blended, the oil will rise to the surface. Put the chicken pieces in the sauce and reheat to serving temperature. Serve with *naan* and a green salad.

Tarka Dhal

Lentils Seasoned with Hot Oil and Spices

Rice and *dhal* are the mainsprings of the working man's diet. In Varanasi, one of India's oldest cities, the god Ganesh is worshipped and special foods prepared from the new harvest for a feast. Later, clay images of him are immersed into the Ganga River and sand from the river bed is sprinkled around the grain stores for his blessing.

6oz/175g/1 cup mixed red lentils (masoor)
and red grain (buwar)
18 fl oz/500ml/3 cups water
$1/2$ tsp turmeric powder
2 whole green chillies, stems removed
1 tsp salt
Seasoning (final fry):
4 tbsp vegetable oil
1 onion, finely sliced
2 cloves garlic, finely sliced
$1/2$ tsp each of mustard, onion and cumin seeds
6 curry leaves
2 whole dry red chillies
1 tsp lemon juice and a few fresh coriander leaves

Pick and wash the *dhals* and drain. Place the first 4 ingredients in a pan and bring to the boil. Lower the heat and simmer with the pan half covered until the *dhals* are soft and most of the water has evaporated. Add salt and mash the *dhals* with a wooden spoon, adjusting the consistency, if too thick, with boiling water. Transfer to a heatproof serving dish and keep warm. In a small frying pan heat the oil and fry the onion and garlic until golden brown. Add the seeds, curry leaves and red chillies and fry for 2–3 minutes. Pour all this over the *dhals*. Sprinkle with lemon juice and coriander leaves and serve.

Balti Jingha Bhendi Masala

Stir Fried Prawn and Okra

Baltistan is far from the sea but it is very fertile and its mountain rivers and lakes provide a good selection of fish and shellfish.

1 1/2 tsp turmeric powder	**Purée:**
1/2 tsp chilli powder (or to taste)	1 large onion, finely chopped
1/2 tsp salt or to taste	1 tsp cumin seeds
1lb/500g raw king prawns, shelled and deveined	1/2 tsp each fennel and fenugreek seeds
4 tbsp oil	3 cloves garlic
4 large tomatoes, finely chopped	1oz/25g fresh ginger
8oz/250g okra, trimmed sparingly	1 tbsp pasanda masala *and* 1 tsp green masala
generous handful of fresh coriander and mint	1 tsp sugar
	1 tsp malt vinegar
	pinch of salt

Mix the first three ingredients and rub into the prawns. Heat the oil and very quickly stir-fry the prawns. Drain from oil and keep aside. In the same oil, fry the purée until you have a well-blended *masala* (about 5 minutes). Add the tomatoes and okra and stir-fry for 5 minutes. Add the prawns, coriander and mint and very gently stir-fry for 5–8 minutes. Serve immediately.

Sarson Jingha

Mustard Spinach with Prawns

The sea-kissed town of Konarak in the state of Orissa is a popular tourist resort. Oriya cuisine depends on seafood and is liberally spiced with mustard — an influence from West Bengal — yet the food has a delectable difference.

---

1 lb/½ kg raw king prawns, shelled and deveined
1 tsp turmeric
salt to taste
4 tsp mustard or vegetable oil
¼ tsp onion seeds (kalonji)
6–8 curry leaves
2 tsp pasanda masala
15oz/450g tinned mustard spinach (sarson)
2 large tomatoes, chopped
handful of fresh coriander leaves

Rub the prawns with the turmeric and salt and keep aside. Heat the oil on medium heat and fry the onion seeds, curry leaves and green masala for 2–3 minutes. Add the prawns and stir-fry until they are bright orange in colour. Fold in the mustard spinach, tomatoes and coriander leaves. Heat to serving temperature and serve with rice or bread.

Xevttallo Molee

Salmon with Chilli-Coconut Sauce

When fresh coconut, chillies and the Manglorean mind fuse, the result is pure culinary magic! Gleaned from the traditional repertoire of this coastal region, here is a classic recipe which displays the ingenuity of yet another genre of Indian cuisine.

1 tsp cumin powder
1 1/2 tsp chilli powder, or to taste
1/2 tsp turmeric powder
1 tbsp wine vinegar
1 1/2 tsp slat or to taste
4–6oz/175g salmon steaks or fillets
4 tbsp vegetable oil
6 fl oz/175ml/1 3/4 cups thick coconut milk (p. 7)
Purée:
1 large onion
6 green chillies
4 cloves garlic
4 in piece fresh ginger
1 1/2 tsp each cumin and coriander powder

Mix the first 5 ingredients into a paste. Coat the salmon thoroughly and marinade for 30 minutes. Heat the oil and fry the puréed ingredients for 5 minutes on medium heat. Add the coconut milk and bring the sauce to the boil. Reduce the heat and gently slip in the salmon. Cook each side in the sauce for 5–8 minutes. Arrange the salmon on a warmed plate and spoon the sauce around them and serve with lemon wedges.

Kotmir Pudina Chutney

Coriander and Mint Relish

An entire book could be written on the chutneys and pickles of India. This has always been my favourite and can be used in many different ways; an accompaniment to any curry or sandwich, or mixed with natural yogurt as a variation to *raitha* (p. 12) or fish filling.

---

2 tbsp vegetable oil
2oz/50g desiccated coconut
2 green chillies and 2 dried red chillies
$^1/_2$ tsp each mustard, cumin, fennel and onion seeds
4 curry leaves
4oz/100g fresh coriander washed and drained
4 tbsp lemon juice
2 tsp mint sauce
salt to taste and 1 tsp sugar

Heat the oil and fry the next 5 ingredients until the coconut is golden brown. Cool the mixture and place in a food processor along with the remaining ingredients. Blend until the coriander is finely chopped. Adjust seasoning and lemon juice if necessary. Serve cold.

Aamba Piyali

Mango Cups

Mango is a very sacred fruit in India. It is said that Lord Shiva brought the mango tree from heaven for his beautiful wife Parvathi whose favourite fruit it was and who had become very upset when she found that mango was not available on earth. Alfonso, Rasdhara, Malgoba and Neelam are some of the Indian mangoes available abroad from Indian grocers between April and July.

---

2 ripe mangoes
4 tsp sugar
1 sachet saffron powder
4 tbsp double cream

Wash the mangoes and dry them gently. Make a cut right through to the seed around the centre of each mango. Hold each mango on both sides of the cut and twist carefully. Two halves will be like cups and the other two will have the seed sticking out. Carefully remove the seeds. Scoop out the inside flesh without damaging the skins. Mash the flesh coarsely and mix in the remaining ingredients. Refill the mango cups with this mixture, chill well and serve. This is very refreshing after a spicy meal.

Shrikhand

Yogurt and Cheese Dessert

Gokulashtmi, the birthday of the Lord Krishna, is celebrated
in honour of his childhood pranks. Earthen pots containing
yogurt, cream and money are suspended from a huge rope on
every street corner. Groups of young boys and men climb on
each other's shoulders to form a human pyramid to reach and
break the pots.

---

4 fl oz/110ml/$\frac{1}{2}$ cup natural yogurt
8oz/225g half-fat cheese
2oz/50g full-fat cheese
2–4 oz/50–100g icing sugar
$\frac{1}{2}$ tsp each ground cardamom and nutmeg
8–10 strands saffron or 1 sachet of powdered saffron
almond flakes and pink rose petals to garnish

Chill a large mixing bowl in the refrigerator for 1 hour. Place
the cheese and yogurt in the bowl and whisk until evenly
mixed. Gradually add the sugar and keep whisking until you
have a light and creamy mixture. Taste as you add the sugar.
You may not wish to use all of it. Add the cardamom, nutmeg
and saffron and mix again. Decorate with the almond flakes
and petals, chill and serve.

Index